Committed
to Grace

Committed
to Grace

Earl and Hazel Lee

Beacon Hill Press of Kansas City
Kansas City, Missouri

Contents

Foreword	7
Preface	9
Acknowledgments	11
1. God Moves in Mysterious Ways	13
2. . . . His Wonders to Perform	18
3. Pilgrimage Toward the Promised Land	22
4. The Hostage Love Story	29
5. The Love Story Continues	33
6. A Bridge over Troubled Waters	38
7. The Homecoming	45
8. Lessons from the Petoskey Stone	52
9. "The Clerk of the Works"	57
10. The Will of God!	61
11. Living with Retirement— a Form of Relinquishment	66
12. The Song Never Ends	72
Notes	79

Foreword

Hazel Lee and I were talking one day about preachers and preaching. I observed that most preachers probably had only one fundamental message in all their different sermons. She quickly responded, "Oh yes! I know Earl has one message—it is commitment."

I think she knows her husband very well. Those of us who have been privileged to know and love the Lees, and to be under their pastoral care have heard from the sermons and received from their lives the message of commitment.

—Commitment to the grace of God. Through all the shared experiences and insights of this book one senses a total reliance of the faithfulness of God's love and mercy; dependency not on self but on grace.

—Commitment to trust in God. Through the shared journey of their lives and ministry they have simply trusted God through whatever good or ill has met them in the way. And they give us now this journal of trust—a sort of handbook on how faith works.

—Commitment to obedience. The simple, radical word is "Yes, Lord." Their "hands down" in surrender have been lifted up in service and ministry stretching around the world. It is plain that their lives have been lived in a continuing "Yes" to the will of God.

Many of us will never read Psalm 37 without reliving the victory cycle of "Commit," "Trust," "Delight," and "Rest." Echoes of these themes are heard all through the reading of this remarkable book. It is not a biography, though we are brought along with them through their experiences of great, great victory and great sorrow. Nor is it a narrative of unusual, eventful, even surprising ministry.

It is more of an inside book—a sort of testament of devotion and obedience. I sense that Hazel and Earl gently lift the veil of events and invite us to look underneath, to look inside, and to perceive the working of the Holy Spirit through their lives and in their ministry.

Through this written witness they have thrown out "an adhesive web of love" (p. 34), and we are caught in it. Caught by the simplicity of their obedience, by the power of their testimony, and by the winsomeness of their lives before us.

—REUBEN R. WELCH
San Diego

Preface

I am writing this chapter in our little mountain home at 6,000-foot altitude on a spring day in April 1992. Earl is at a retreat in Colorado Springs with the Nazarene Bible College graduating class. I am enjoying some "thinking time"—physically alone but filled with the awareness of God's presence.

I have just been rereading some of the chapters already written for this book. It is a bit tricky to write and speak and travel, and one fears incoherence as well as irrelevance. I ask myself, Why are we writing this book? Why add another book to the full tide already on the market? Well, for one thing, we felt that special nudge of the Holy Spirit to put some of our experiences into print, since we wrote *The Cycle of Victorious Living* 20 years ago. It seems to be in demand even now as a "testament of devotion." But we have experienced the living reality of Psalm 37 in our lives during some demanding years since 1971. The call of God to commit, trust, delight, and rest has been a part of our daily living.

We write to encourage and inspire many who also are pilgrims on the King's Highway, who need to go "from strength to strength," as the Psalmist says. We join hands with you in the common knowledge that Jesus is Lord, and along the way we find oases, pools of living water, and the Rock of Ages in a weary land.

John Henry Jowett writes, "Nothing so rekindles hope as a journey through the mercies of yesterday."[1] Like the story of Hansel and Gretel, we would drop crumbs of comfort for these who follow after us or along with us. Jesus never fails! And so *avanti,* as the Italians say. Straight ahead to the gates of pearl!

The following chapters contain highlights from our years of ministry. Perhaps they would be like mountain peaks soaring above the whole range of mountains. In this type of writing there are long pauses. This book is not a biography, but more like separate scenes taken from many pages of script.

The title of our book comes from a sermon Earl preached not too long ago from Acts 14:26 in the *New International Version.* Paul was returning to Antioch, where he had worked previously in seeking to strengthen the disciples and encourage them to be true to the faith. When he arrived back at Antioch he greeted the disciples who had been "committed to the grace of God for the work they had now completed."

In a way, that's what we did as we left our beloved church and headed out into the unknown. Therefore, the song "Amazing Grace" took on a new meaning for us those days, as well as these succeeding years of serving where God opens doors.

> *Thro' many dangers, toils, and snares*
> *I have already come.*
> *'Tis grace hath bro't me safe thus far,*
> *And grace will lead me home.*

—HAZEL LEE

Acknowledgments

How do you say "Thank you" strongly enough to the Holy Spirit for His gentle nudgings toward a particular task? The more He impressed on our hearts to write this sequel to *The Cycle of Victorious Living,* the less convenient it became. The interruptions of traveling and speaking have been legion, interfering with streams of thought that had to be laid aside for more convenient seasons. We have found that God's directives do not often fit into our preconceived pattern for living. So over a period of a year we have sought to follow through.

We are surprised but are most grateful to our Nazarene Publishing House for taking the risk of publishing our book and for Bonnie Perry, our editorial coordinator.

Thank you, Reuben Welch, for your willingness to contribute our foreword from your own expertise and loving friendship.

We shall ever be grateful to our dear friend, Betty Corbin, for her consistent encouragement when we would faint by the wayside. We thank her also for her patient, long-suffering typing of our manuscript pages.

May this "missile of grace" bless those of you who are interested enough to read, and, in reading, may you discover new shoes for the road.

Chapter 1

God Moves
in Mysterious Ways

It was 1959, and we were concluding 14 years in India as missionaries with the tremendous responsibility of being superintendent to these very special people of the Church of the Nazarene. The language was ours—Marathi. We loved the people of our area and the church. Our family was secure in this land, so all seemed clear for another seven-year term of ministry after our upcoming furlough to the States.

Then came the trip from Basim to Mehekar, where we were stationed. I have lived all my life listening to "the still small voice." The stanzas in our lives have been marked by the command, "This is the way; walk in it" (Isa. 30:21). But this could be quite disruptive. Alone in my Plymouth station wagon, with the dust whirling around me as I pushed on about 40 miles per hour, came His voice! "When you return home for your furlough—stay there. Do not return to India."

It is impossible to explain what this meant. A missionary is a very secure person, especially one backed by the Church of the Nazarene. My response as I drove was "One does not do this. What will my fellow missionaries say? What will the General Board in Kansas City think and say?"

I was soon driving down the long driveway to our bungalow in Mehekar. After a while, in a relaxed moment, I realized I would be sharing with Hazel this very unusual thought. Over this path of more than 50 years together, we have claimed that unique verse in Matt. 18:19—"Again, I tell you that if two of you on earth agree about anything you ask for, it will be done for you by my Father in heaven." Certainly we were at a major crossroad in our lives, and we must have agreement.

I shared with Hazel this unusual experience that had just transpired. My wife's first reaction was not unexpected as she said, "I can't see where this could be God's will for us. No doubt the pressures of the field are getting to you. You have a right to be tired. It seems we are only now getting ready [after 14 years] to be of more adequate service to Christ here in India."

I quickly agreed and cast aside the impression. But in my spirit, the thought persisted—and I have learned that the still small voice has a way of persisting if it is His voice.

"Is the matter of our returning home for good still before you as you mentioned a few weeks ago?" Hazel asked me.

I answered, "Yes it is, and just as clear." For I had been facing some personal questions associated with a form I had to fill out for the government of India relative to my work and the application to return. It was known as a Residential Permit to Return to India. Included were questions such as "How long have you been in India?" "What is your major purpose of work?" "Are you training anyone to take your place?" Right here I had to admit, "Yes, I have been training Indian pastors to take my place"—and then the punch line: "When will they be ready?" With honesty, I had to admit with joy, "They are ready now." This meant removing myself from the overall picture as chairman of the India District and letting the very capable Indian personnel move on. Yes, they had been preparing for far more than two generations and needed to be thrust into total and complete leadership. Therefore, with this background, our discussion in the quietness of our much-loved home in the heart of our district—and almost in the heart of this land of India—was extremely important.

The outcome of hours of talking together and praying, with no effort of either of us to convince the other, was the quiet decision to return to the States with our three children and begin to reshape our lives. Gary, 16, was planning for college. Gayle, 13, was about to go into high school. Grant, our youngest (born in India), was ready for grade school at 10 years of age.

Before we left India, in God's providence and with permission from the General Board, we spent a year as chaplain of the school in Kodai Kanal, South India, where our three children were in attendance. The beautiful plus of this assignment was getting back to opening the Word again as a pastor, without the demands of administration. It was a delightful year for us as a family, giving us many opportunities to meet people from around the world of many denominations and backgrounds. Our parsonage by the lovely lake at 7,000-foot altitude was a restful gift from our Heavenly Father.

With our older son's interest in geology and the Science Department at Northwest Nazarene College, we faced another traumatic decision as we planned to go to Nampa, Idaho, rather than to the East Coast, where Hazel and I received our college education at Eastern Nazarene College. It meant going into a completely unknown place to live, with very few acquaintances and no assurance of a house, furniture, or car. It meant disappointing loved ones in the East. It was a wrenching decision, but we had the quiet assurance this was God's leading. *Commit—trust—delight—rest* was becoming a vital part of our new direction in life in our early 40s.

After a long journey by ship, we were met in Los Angeles by my sister, Hazel's mother, and a college friend. We were literally in unknown territory. No one else knew us, and we knew no one else; but bit by bit, all of our immediate needs were met.

I settled the family into the school year and began my deputation work. With a family to provide for, no special plans ahead, and with the knowledge I was not to return to India, I kept pleading for God to show me His future for our lives. One day as I was walking the streets of Duncan, Okla., at my wit's end, I prayed—"Lord, I want to know Your will. You have brought us back to the States; I am doing my deputation assignment, but what next?"

Looking back on it now I realize my ego was at stake. I felt like a very stupid person. "All right, Lord, please—*Your* will." Then the word came. Of course, it was quiet, direct, and quite simple. It was the "pivot point"—"You have my will for *today!*" It was the same whisper from my Heavenly Father who had said in 1959, "Go home to the States and stay there."

I was rather taken aback with the reply, but with it came a deep peace and, to God be the glory, Hazel had the same experience at about the same time in Nampa. Again, "If two of you shall agree . . ." Now I couldn't wait until the next friend would ask me what we were going to do for the future—and to smile and say, "Oh! We have God's will for today." The response was always the same: "Yes, I know that, but . . ." Again, God was teaching us to trust Him.

Another major pivot point was in the office of a general leader of our church in Kansas City. He was greatly troubled that we were not returning to India and in his own unique way put all the pressure he could on us to say yes and return. Then, in futility, he pointed his well-experienced finger at me (I was his much-loved friend) and said words that remain in my mind to this moment—"Earl, I want you to know that with this decision, you have lost all influence with missionaries and on mission fields." I had no debate and quietly replied, "I know this, Sir," and with a handshake I went out of his office and left Kansas City. After visiting relatives in the East, we went west to live in Nampa, Idaho, on a completely new track in our lives.

Nampa!—six wonderful years as pastor of one of the finest congregations anywhere. They gave me the privilege of learning to preach regularly again after 14 years as a missionary in India. Idaho was the ideal place to spend a lifetime. My age was right—42; our children were in the right place; and the church was alive and exciting. Here, we thought, we would settle down.

And then the phone rang. It is similar to the story in Luke 8:41: *"Then* a man named Jairus . . . ,"* and life was changed. The call was from a friend in California, the Los Angeles district superintendent. He broached a question that changed my life, as well as the lives of my family members and many other people: "Earl, would you consider accepting a call to be pastor of Pasadena First Church?" Idaho we loved, especially Nampa First Church, but deep down I felt God's will was California.

For the family the transition was not easy—Gayle with a wedding in a few months, Gary off to the Army, and Grant having to leave a small high school with a first-class band to enter a large, impersonal high school with a withering band program. Yet at a timely breakfast with just him and me, I asked his opinion of the invitation to California. He was a part of a great youth group at Nampa First with his youth pastor and our friend, Dee Freeborn, a true mentor. After we talked and I assured him we would not make the change if he declined, his words were penetrating— "Dad, if God calls *you,* He calls *me!*" And so, with a spirit of trust and rest, we turned ourselves toward California. It was a tearful decision. We did not understand God's pattern; we knew only to obey.

Chapter 2

. . . His Wonders to Perform

Earl and I believe that in life there seems to be a divine crescendo—one experience builds on another. How often have I heard Earl say in a message that "God is a God of economy." He doesn't waste anything or any experience we go through. He taught us many disciplines while in India that we could have learned in no other way.

The six years of pastoring before we went to India prepared us in many ways to trust and then delight when material needs were met only through faith and prayer. The happy years in Nampa gave us time to be a united family in a thriving church. When in India, our children had been deprived of the joy of a church that sang and spoke the Word in their own language, plus a vital youth program. In Nampa they had that. I enjoyed the privilege of teaching a fine college Sunday School class in English, not Marathi, which I had to use in India. We went to Pasadena quite seasoned through numerous joys and sorrows.

I like what George Watson once said: "God never prepares half a providence any more than man makes half a pair of scissors." Throughout these years of service He was preparing us for the beautiful tape ministry that evolved throughout our years of pastoring in Pasadena. How often we thought of the words of our Kansas City friend, who in all good faith had said, "Earl, you will have no more influence on the mission field if you do not return." When we left Pasadena, our tape ministry had reached out to over 90 countries, 45 different denominations, as 3,000 tapes a week were mailed out by the volunteer effort of our dedicated tape ministry staff. Earl was truly a missionary/pastor here in the States, as well as abroad. The following is his story of the unfolding of the tape ministry, surely one of the reasons God led us to Pasadena First Church.

Like many other churches at that time, we had the large reel-to-reel tape recorder for recording the church services. This ministry was maintained by a group of dedicated laymen who saw that the best was done for the few who received the tapes during the week. This ministry touched a total of perhaps 12 shut-ins or those in hospitals. The entire service was taped and then brought to these eager listeners. How they appreciated this loving service!

One of the faithful listeners ministered to by the tape ministry was hospitalized with terminal cancer. One day as I went to visit her, she told us she had let Jesus into her heart after hearing the tape and that she wanted to be baptized, take Communion, be anointed, and join the church. It was such a joy to follow the requests of this lovely, cultured, and educated lady. This was all taken care of one afternoon after she returned home. It was a beautiful experience. Her husband had quietly but decisively come back to the Lord after some years of wandering away.

In a matter of months, it was apparent the cancer had returned; yet the joy of the Lord Jesus was hers, and it was a lift to be in her presence. She went back to the hospital, where medicine and doctors did all they could. Finally, it was her wish to return to her home for her last days. Every week faithful friends brought the tapes to her home. That large, heavy case with the 8" reel was her spiritual lift every week. Weakness took its toll, and then she asked her husband, "When I am gone, please use our money to give the church an adequate tape ministry with the best equipment possible." In a few days she was in heaven— perfectly healed for eternity.

Her husband did exactly as his wife had asked, and

before long we had the best taping equipment available for the beginning of the "Cassettes for Christ" ministry, which was to reach around the world like an ever-widening, richer, fuller stream.

It was a Sunday in 1968, two years after we went to Pasadena, that our new equipment was used for the first time by the same dedicated laymen who worked into the early-morning hours to prepare the first mailing of 35 tapes. We agreed the tape was to include all the music as well as the sermon. I feel that was one of the reasons the tapes became such a blessing, especially to those far from home on lonely mission stations. These first tapes were sent to servicemen and missionaries from our local church.

It wasn't long before people were writing and asking how to get the tapes, and we made the decision—a major step of faith—to mail them free to home mission pastors who asked for them, as well as missionaries anywhere in the world. Realizing how vital the messages were becoming, we airmailed the tapes, suggesting they be passed on. How often since that time we have heard of shoeboxes full of tapes in various places, somewhat like a lending library around the world.

Before we moved to our new sanctuary, I became accustomed during the half hour before the Sunday evening service to reading letters we had received from around the world, giving the stamps to children who collected them. I also enjoyed playing my trumpet during that time. It was a very colorful half hour, and the church was usually full by service time.

As I look back over those years, what can I say? My heart is filled with joy at the unexpected surprises of God through the obedience of that dear lady and her husband.

In time, these tapes made their way to Russia, China (in the Canadian diplomatic pouch), and Saudi Arabia (where they were used for worship among people gathering for services on Friday, the Holy Day in a Muslim country). Nurses in the Sudan were blessed as they worshiped and then, in turn, let new converts listen. They even gained entrance into Tehran, Iran, because a Bell Helicopter employee who was a Nazarene had asked for the tapes. This brother told me of their blessing and wrote often from Iran—where our Gary was a prisoner for 444 days. Our friend escaped from Iran just after the Shah left; yet he told me he gave several shoeboxes filled with "Cassettes for Christ" to Iranian Christians as he left. I have often wondered what happened to those lives. We will meet in heaven.

It was a special joy for us to plan a "Cassettes for Christ" breakfast during the 1976 General Assembly. Missionaries, as well as others from around the world, came to share what a blessing the tapes had been. I was especially moved to hear how they used the Communion service we sent in dry form. The juice had to be Kool-aid—I think the Lord must have smiled over that substitution. It was also a special privilege for them to meet the committee who worked so faithfully on the tapes. People who had been only names became faces. These small tapes were indeed little missiles of grace as First Church continually sowed seeds.

As said in the beginning of this chapter, we had no idea once again how God's divine crescendo was working in our lives. These tapes became the forerunners of the past eight years of our so-called retirement. We would never have had invitations to speak in Africa, Europe, Taiwan, Brazil, New Zealand, New Guinea, Australia, Hawaii, Canada, as well as all over America, if it had not been for this extra ministry from Pasadena First Church. To God be the glory—great things He has done.

Chapter 3

Pilgrimage
Toward the Promised Land

We often called the first 10 years of our ministry in Pasadena our "journey toward the Sunrise Campus," since we were moving east from our other church location. Our slogan for those years was "straight ahead," as well as "Yes, Lord." Why would a pastor seek to see a congregation move from one vicinity to another with all the ramifications, inevitable grumblings, huge financial demands, and outside pressures? For one thing, the congregation itself was the moving force. We were running out of room in the sanctuary and lacked parking spaces. Growth has its own problems, as well as its challenges. After many meetings and studying possible ways we might handle the problem, it was finally decided to move out and move on.

In my little booklet "The Saga of the Pepper Tree," which gives details of these years, Hazel shares her reactions of what the move would demand of me. By the way, the pepper tree was the tree under which the staff prayed and claimed the property for our new church if God so willed. It is still on the campus.

Here are Hazel's words:

There were two on the Emmaus Road. Quite probably a husband and wife—sorrowing, confused, disappointed.

The "Alongside One" revealed himself in His own

time and they gazed in wonder at each other as they said, "Didn't our hearts burn within us while He talked with us along the way?"

Earl and I have shared all major decisions in our lives in a unified and harmonious and mutually-agreed manner. The decision to take on the huge task of relocation was not to my liking. I feared the load would be too heavy and I did not want Earl to succumb to the challenge. It was a difficult time for him as well as for me.

After much prayer and searching of my own heart I had to be willing to relinquish and trust. It was very difficult for me. Even after the plans were drawn up and the move was in progress, we met difficulty after difficulty. But I had learned during our years as missionaries in India that one can be in God's perfect will and find everything seem to go wrong! That inner assurance of God saying, "This is the way—walk in it" (I'm glad He did not say run in it) is a great steadying factor.

One Saturday morning when things were very dark, I sat alone on the patio praying and thinking, when the Comforter drew near again and brought renewal. He also seemed to inspire a poetic thought in my heart which I wrote down for our encouragement in the following words:

My Promised Land

Because I can see nothing,
I am committed to the God who does the impossible,
"The over-and-above-all" I can ask or think,
Who delights in performing miracles!

He sent a whale to carry Jonah to obedience,
A dove to encourage Noah's faith,
A cloud in answer to Elijah's prayer,
And a fire to prove He was Jehovah, the Mighty One.

He takes everyday things to confound the mighty,
And His ways are past finding out.

If He took a piece of clay to heal the blind,
A little fish to feed the multitudes,
A touch of His finger to restore Life,
A look to break a heart,
And a nail to redeem the world,
Can He not take a little grain of mustard seed faith
And move a mountain?

I believe . . . *I BELIEVE.*

And so we moved forward with our hands joined in faith. When the Expansion Committee heard the price tag for the property we had prayed about under the pepper tree, our hearts sank. We had combed the vicinity of Pasadena to find some land that would be appropriate, and this was the only piece we felt would accommodate our plans. It looked impossible, and in the midst of the death of our vision, we knew God's way for all of us was to commit, trust, delight, and rest. We rested in the Lord with an alert faith. The problem became His, as it would over and over again.

Not long after committing this dream to the Lord, I heard Pasadena College was planning to move to San Diego. At first it was hearsay, but soon enough I found out it was a reality. That meant that we would lose about 150 fine families out of our congregation—at least 300 people. That would also mean we need not move, and we would have the challenge of a community church to fill the vacancies with new people. God marvelously answered our prayers, and in time the church was filled again. We were having three Sunday morning services, the parking lot was woefully inadequate, and the property we had looked at years before was still not sold.

We were in the midst of many problems. We heard the property we wanted was offered at a price of $420,000, far beyond anything we could even imagine paying. But over a period of time we made a successful bid (that in itself was a miracle), and we had accumulated $160,000 toward a down payment. However, we needed another $260,000 or so to finish off our payment.

In the fall of 1974 my wife and I took our little trailer and went up into the mountains for a vacation. How we enjoyed God's beautiful world—walking, talking, praying, sitting by the fire at night under the stars. We were quiet in our spirits, quiet enough to hear God's gentle whispers. His whisper may have been gentle, but one day it burned a hole into my heart. Could I have been hearing correctly? The message that came to me that cool autumn day was "If we are to do such a mammoth and impossible task as building a church on those 12 acres, we had better begin by doing the impossible and paying for the entire property in *cash!*" When I mentioned this to Hazel, she was dumbfounded. We both agreed it was a supreme challenge, but we were committed to the God of the impossible.

When we returned to the parsonage that weekend, I spent time writing my message to the church to be read the following Sunday morning. It would mean a complete revision of all the plans for raising money, plans the Finance Committee had put in motion. I had to meet with them first before I shared with the congregation. Feeling puzzled and apprehensive, the committee trusted me enough to feel the message was God's message for the time. The congregation was stunned at first, but they, too, accepted the challenge and the excitement of seeing what God had in store for us.

The wheels began to turn. People brought in money throughout the week. Our target date was November 17, 1974—only three weeks away. There was an aura of breathless excitement building up in all the services. Some of my fine laymen wanted to have a backup plan in case not all the money came in, but I did not feel that would be honoring our faith, so we agreed to set it aside and trust God.

If ever I felt like Moses leading the Israelites through the Red Sea, I did on that Sunday morning. I forgot who said it, but I found assurance in the quote, "God, give me a task too big, too hard for human hands; then I shall come at length to lean on Thee, and leaning, find my strength." As I stepped into the pulpit that morning, believe me—I was leaning on the Lord.

That Sunday will ever be a victorious memory of Pasadena First Church's history as at the close of the day we exceeded our goal by $10,000. God supplied over and above, and the congregation, with a full blast from the organ, rejoiced with tears and shouts of praise in an unforgettable burst of thanksgiving to our God, who always honors faith. Indeed, faith in God *did* move a mighty mountain.

After a few days the property was ours. Every roadblock was miraculously removed, and we placed our sign on the property near the highway—"Future Home of the Church of the Nazarene." Our slogan again was "Straight Ahead."

On July 4, 1976, we broke ground with flags flying and hearts rejoicing in what God had helped us do. God knew how much we would need the memories of November 17 and July 4 as we began the long journey through the desert of disappointments, including a stop-work order from the City Council because of an antagonistic neighbor's complaint and floods produced by unseasonal rains, damaging some homes downhill from our construction. It seemed it was one thing after another.

In the midst of it all, our son Gary was taken captive in Iran November 4, 1979, and we faced a year of intense heartache over that situation. (This experience is related in subsequent chapters.) In 1972, before we started our promised-land pilgrimage, we had committed ourselves to the great commission of sowing seeds away from ourselves. We had pledged as a church to help the Lamb's Church of the Nazarene get started in Manhattan, New York City.

With all our personal financial needs, we were still able to invest over $100,000 in the Lamb's Church, as well as providing personnel who took their own time and money to assist in various ways as needed. To God be the glory for the great things He did during those crucial days.

Recently we received a huge carton through United Parcel Service. We couldn't imagine what was in it. After opening the box and pulling out reams of bubble material, we lifted out a beautifully framed picture of the Lamb's Church in Manhattan. A few months ago we visited them for their 18th anniversary. This lovely picture is a call to prayer for this corner of light in a very dark area. Pasadena First Church, learning to sow seeds away from itself, was a part of the planting operation.

During the 10 years of expansion at Pasadena a fine group of dedicated Christians met each Friday morning from 6:00 to 7:00 without fail. I feel every church needs this "central heating system," and "Early Christians" was our place to bring prayer requests. I wrote the requests on a chalkboard, and then we prayed. It was a real support group for me, and I always left that hour feeling uplifted as I went into our regular weekly staff meeting.

I am writing these thoughts in 1991. It is a joy to reminisce on the faithfulness of God. It has been seven years this month since I retired from the active pastorate and moved into a new dimension of service. As I review my life, I am still amazed at the timings of God. Although I wrote the following lines in 1980, I find they are just as true for me today:

> Right on time,
> God does His work
> In us and through us.
>
> When we thought He was silent,
> He was at work.
>
> When our next step was in darkness,
> The light appeared.

When we had to turn to the right or left,
His direction was clear.

When our plan was vetoed by Him,
He had a better one.

Never early but never late,
Right on time,
God does His work
In us and through us.

    Amen and Amen.

Chapter 4

The Hostage Love Story

The very title seems to be a contradiction—"Hostage—
Love." Somewhere in these words has to be a miracle:
"A natural or supernatural event with precise timing that
brings glory to God."

Life changed for the Lee family November 4, 1979. It
was a normal Sunday morning. I was to serve early Communion, as was our custom the first Sunday of the month.
I was greeting the early comers in the narthex when a
brother asked me if I had heard the news on the radio. My
answer was no, for the world news and the Good News
did not have much in common for a preacher on Sunday
morning.

"The news says terrorists have overrun the American
Embassy in Tehran and that all our personnel have been
taken captive," he said. "Isn't your son Gary in Iran?" And
life has never been the same since.

The early days of the captivity were filled with apprehension, questions, and even anticipation. But then the daily drudgery of the "long haul" set in.

I had determined I would not fall prey to the media.
In December a request for an interview had come from a
reporter for the *Pasadena Star News*. The phone call came to
the parsonage, and Hazel, knowing how strongly I felt,
turned her down. But as the reporter heard Hazel's reply,
she closed her request by simply saying, "I have recently
read his book, *The Cycle of Victorious Living*, and I wonder if
it is working now. Do you mind if I call back?"

When I arrived home that evening, Hazel relayed the conversation with the reporter to me, and I replied, "No way!" Then Hazel dropped the last line, "She wonders if it works now." My answer was right to the point: "I give up." In a few days this reporter was in our home, and her interview with me was well done. As she was leaving, she thanked me, shook my hand, smiled, and said, "Six months ago I let Jesus Christ into my heart."

The next day the Lee family and the story about our son Gary in Iran was public news to our city of over 100,000.

Now to return to normal and refuse further media intrusions. But then an NBC reporter crept in the "back door" through a member of our church. Janine Tartaglia, weekend anchor for NBC, heard psychologists discussing the possible mental health of the hostages on their return home whenever they did return. Sam Mayhugh was on the panel discussing the subject, and he mentioned that one of the hostages was known to him and that the hostage's father was his pastor. This was all Janine needed. She got my name, our son Gary's name, and with clever maneuvering had the agreement for a "brief" TV interview in our home.

Little did we dream what God had in mind. The TV invasion went well. After the cameras were off, a casual conversation began the friendship between Janine and our family. Enter Grandma Estelle Crutcher, Hazel's mother, then age 84. As the TV invasion was being carried on in our living room, Mrs. Crutcher was seated in a distant corner of the room, watching everything. That evening, Janine was on the evening news with her report on Gary Lee and the Lee family hostage story.

Although the family had decided to go public, I was still determined to limit our media involvement. There is quite a struggle in the journey of love. Does one select when he should love? Does one love conditionally? No! Of course, when Jesus steps into the middle of our lives and we take Him seriously, all changes. We could wish Jesus would come in person when groups and individuals like the media come into our lives. Yet only when He comes through us and our humanness will He appear in our world.

It was that way April 25, 1980. The attempted rescue had been made by the U.S. Air Force planes and heli-copters. As well planned as it was, an unusually strong sandstorm came as eight helicopters were ready to fly to-ward Tehran to rescue our men and women who were held captive. Eight of our airmen perished in the desert sands.

An "All-Day Time for Prayer" had been planned for this day months before, just to observe good discipline and to fast and pray. The TV friends were present at church, au-diting "a story." Janine, with the TV camera crew, watched all day. A devout Catholic, she talked with the church folk. She even asked to go into the church to observe their quiet prayer. She observed firm smiles expressing hope and con-fidence. All of this was a part of the penetration of love.

During these weeks and months there was very little communication with our son Gary—or any other of the 52 Americans. We learned later that after the attempted res-cue they were scattered over many places in Iran.

Now came January 1981. Rumors were rampant: "The hostages will be released." "Money is to be transferred." "Algeria is in the heart of the negotiations." But we had been on so many yo-yos that we steeled ourselves against too much hope.

January 16 was Friday. Hazel was in northern Califor-nia speaking to a ladies' retreat. I was returning from San Diego, where I had been speaking to the student body at Point Loma Nazarene College. The Lord had allowed me to speak on *The Cycle of Victorious Living* for the first time in 14 months. My previous assignment was to live it. I had planned dinner out with Hazel's mother. I called from the church to the parsonage, asking my brother-in-law, Lowell, to bring "Gram" Crutcher to me so that we could go to eat.

I was told, "No way! The media has surrounded this house. They are everywhere—front door and back door." Soon Irma, Lowell's wife, came to the phone to confirm—"No way out!" I replied, "I'll be right home."

I was disgusted with the media for controlling our lives. I quickly left the church office and began the three-mile drive to the parsonage. I must admit that my stomach was twisted into an emotional pretzel. My knuckles were white, and I was anything but relaxed. Really, I was no example of *The Cycle of Victorious Living*. At about the halfway mark toward the parsonage the still, small voice again changed my life with that clear whisper—"Love them. Love them in My place."

The voice was familiar. Only one answer would satisfy, and it was an immediate "Yes, Lord!" I relaxed. The knuckles regained their color, and the last mile passed quickly. Sure enough, the media was everywhere. Lights, cameras, trucks, but mostly people—all the networks. With ease I drove into the back driveway and sauntered over to them with a smile and a warm hello. They were surprised at my relaxed courtesy. Microphones flew into position (three inches from my nose), and we proceeded to talk. Questions and answers—it was fun. No tensions; love was freed. After 30 minutes of this media exercise, I asked, "May I take my mother-in-law to dinner?"

Thinking they were in charge, they gleefully answered, "Yes, you may go now!" We all laughed as I entered the parsonage and announced to "Grams," "We may go now." Love works both ways to bring a relaxed atmosphere. Really, the media thought *we* were the captives. Actually *they* were now captured by love.

Chapter 5

The Love Story Continues

G randma Crutcher and I proceeded to a favorite restaurant for our evening meal. I was amazed at how many people had already seen my interview on TV. They commented on my message and thanked me for the spirit of the interview. I, in turn, thanked God for nudging me to love and not resist.

When we returned to the parsonage, all 75 correspondents—with various equipment—were still there. But since there were no barriers between us, the atmosphere was relaxed.

It was a cold January evening, and I invited them into the parsonage. They seemed reluctant, but Janine, right in the middle of them, waved them in with a jovial "Come on, fellas" and led them in, and Grandma and I entertained. They really did not need to be entertained. It was fun. Stan played the piano. What food we had was soon devoured. Grams was the center of attention with her confident words, "My grandson is coming home—praise the Lord."

The usual 10 P.M. and 11 P.M. news broadcasts were made right from our living room, with all the networks and the independent stations. Grams went to bed, and a few minutes after 11:30 P.M. I excused myself, and all our media friends were off. What a day! January 16, 1981— Love was the winner.

Saturday was the usual quiet day awaiting Sunday. Yet at 8 A.M. "they" were at the door. I greeted them with a casually pleasant, "What are you here for today? Nothing is going to happen today." Yet they persisted—"You can never tell"—and asked permission to go over to the church with me. Of course, the request was granted.

The key question was asked by David Dow of CBS: "May we come to church Sunday morning?" I replied with a happy "Yes" to all our friends. I had to add a loving barb, "Sure, come. The center of the balcony is yours—the service might do you some good."

Again, it seemed such a small matter. After all the media left, only one person remained—our NBC "anchor lady," Janine Tartaglia. She lingered and came into my office. "May I visit with you, Pastor?" "Of course—have a seat" was my relaxed response.

Then began another pivotal conversation with this lovely lady in the process of being captured by the love of God. Days before, from the first meeting of Janine and Grandma Crutcher, a rare bond began forming. It was as Leo Tolstoy said: "The means to gain happiness is to throw out from oneself, like a spider, in all directions, an adhesive web of love, and to catch in it all that comes."

As a result of God's loving web on January 17, 1981, Janine expressed deep feelings she could not understand. "Pastor, something or someone is drawing me. I have been seeing God's love as I have never seen it. God seems to be drawing me to himself. What do you advise?"

For sure, we do not need to hasten the pace of the grace of God. My answer seemed too simple, yet I was comfortable as I replied, "Janine, just say 'Yes, Lord.'" So began Janine's journey of surrender.

Please remember that during this momentous time Hazel was in northern California speaking at a ladies' retreat. In a private "deal" with God she insisted she did not want to miss the release of Gary from his prison in Iran and the joy that would be in abundance. The Lord assured her, "You will not miss a thing." Nor did she.

Then came Sunday, January 18. The church, nearly

completed and seating 2,500 people, was packed. Excitement was in the air. The choir exploded with the great choral presentation "Rejoice, Rejoice—My Son Is Coming Home Again." Before the prayer, we asked those wearing prayer bracelets to come forward and place them on the altar as thanksgiving to God and a declaration of faith that our hostages were in the process of gaining their freedom. It was a deeply touching moment. The pastoral prayer was direct from heaven to this pastor's heart.

In the midst of the congregational singing, there was a personal transaction taking place in the balcony, where more than 75 media friends were recording and reporting on the feeling and flow of this service, which was being broadcast and televised nationwide and worldwide. God and Janine had a private "word" in the midst of all the happenings. When the congregation was seated, I looked into the balcony, and there was Janine standing all alone. She seemed oblivious to all of the hundreds around her.

Later that day she shared with me: "Pastor, it was very clear that God said to me, 'Janine, put down your note pad and pencil. I want you!'" Then quietly she said with great emotion, "I did—and now what do I do?"

With a smile and yet a deep "Thank You, Lord" in my heart I said, "Say 'Yes, Lord'—and go talk to Grandma Crutcher!"

Janine faced some mountain-sized decisions. It was a series of surrenders. It all sounded like the statement by William James: "The whole development of Christianity or its inwardness consists in little more than greater and greater emphasis on the crisis of surrender."

One afternoon Janine and Mrs. Crutcher had a time together in the parsonage living room. Again Janine faced a "yes" or "no" to a television contract with considerable financial security. At the same time, the undeniable call of God to His ministry was there. Mrs. Crutcher, then about 84 years young, knew only one path—very direct. "Janine, you must die out to television and money and all it means and say a surrendered 'Yes' to God. Now you kneel at this coffee table and settle it."

Janine did! Janine said a total surrendered "Yes" to God, and life was then "straight ahead."

She soon resigned from KNBC, but they requested her to host a program once a week called "Odyssey." This was a popular program aimed at personal interviews of various life interests and beliefs. Janine is an excellent interviewer.

Then the pursuit for ministry—it was my joy to ask her to join the pastoral staff at First Church, and she accepted the portfolio of "Pastor to Senior Adults." She was tailor-made for the position. Her eight years of adventure in this ministry would be a book in itself.

Now it was a case of "no looking back." Her baptism was beautiful, with her family coming from San Luis Obispo, 100 miles north. She entered the pastor's class for membership and enjoyed it. With several others, she joined the First Church of the Nazarene.

Janine was heading straight for ordination. She worked on the Home Course of Study, as well as a master's degree in religion at Azusa Pacific University. At Azusa she was one lady among 12 men in the master's program, all ministers from various denominations. Janine closed those very valuable two years with a straight-A average, and, although only five feet tall, she was heart to heart with the entire class.

Ordination was blessed for Janine, with a church filled with friends as well as many family members. She became a minister of the gospel in the Church of the Nazarene.

With her trusty guitar and her heart filled with God's love, Janine is traveling as an evangelist—yes, a revivalist—with the Church of the Nazarene, as well as other denominations, truly demonstrating God's love in action. Her heartfelt message is God's desire for a holy people. This whole story is a testament to the truth that love never fails.

Now we look back: 1979, Iran, hostages, pain, tears,

questions, new people in our lives, freedom for Gary and 51 others, great joy, and the miracle of love! For through Janine the end is eternal.

I am reminded of Joseph's story in Genesis. He was a hostage and suffered a great deal. Yet when the summation was being made, he said to his family and those who had intended him great harm, "You intended to harm me, but God intended it for good to accomplish what is now being done, the saving of many lives. So then, don't be afraid" (Gen. 50:20). To God be the glory!

Chapter 6

A Bridge over Troubled Waters

I find a haunting truth in the song "Bridge Over Troubled Waters." I couple it with the statement by Arthur John Gossip: "When life tumbles in—what then?" He spoke of the death of his wife, but it could be applied to any unexpected crisis in our lives, such as a situation that we cannot foresee that pounces on us unawares.

Sunday morning, November 4, 1979, began as any Sunday in a parsonage. Earl had gone to church early to serve "volunteer" Communion around the tables in front of the sanctuary. This occasion was very special, served once a month for those who cared to come early. I was alone in the parsonage since my mother, who lived with us during those years in Pasadena, was in Atlanta visiting one of my brothers.

As I sat by the fire reviewing my Sunday School lesson, the phone rang. When I answered it, I was surprised to hear Earl's voice. When he said, "I'm afraid I have bad news for you," my mind flew in many directions, but especially toward Atlanta and my mother. I was completely unprepared for his following statement: "I have been told by one of the members coming in for Communion that terrorists have overrun the embassy in Tehran and all the personnel have been taken hostage. The news came to him over the radio."

My immediate response was, "Oh, that means Gary!" My mind reeled as my body shook.

"Shall I come home?" he asked. I told him to go on

serving Communion and I would be all right. I walked back to the fireplace, sat down, and said to God, "If ever I needed a promise from Your Word, I need it now." I simply opened my Bible, not knowing where to look, and I turned to a couple of phrases in Isa. 60:9: "to bring thy sons from far . . . unto the name of the Lord" (KJV). I felt as though a warm thermal blanket had been placed around my shoulders, and I knew the wonderful comfort of the Holy Spirit.

He entered, by what secret stair,
I know not—
Only knowing *he was there!*

I turned on the radio and heard a reporter from Los Angeles interviewing one of the terrorists. He asked if one of the hostages could come to the phone and speak to the American people to let us know they were alive. The request was refused. As I turned the radio off, my one thought was that they were all dead. (We did not have any assurance for three more weeks that Gary was alive.) I entered into the dark night of the soul, when it always seems to be three o'clock in the morning. I did not feel brave—I was frightened—but I knew exactly where to turn in an hour of deep need. My prayer was, "Lord, what do I do next?" My desire was to stay alone and compose my inner self.

But the Holy Spirit, the greatest of all psychologists, knew exactly what I needed to do. It was as though He put His hand under my chin, lifted my face up, and said four simple words—"Do the next thing." Was I hearing correctly? How could I dress, go to church, take Communion, and teach my Sunday School class with this heavy weight of grief in my heart? Yet this directive from the Holy Spirit was the very bridge I needed over those troubled waters. Thank God I had no idea it would be a long 444 days before I got to the other side.

One thing I had learned throughout my years of following my Lord was to obey *no matter how I felt.* Too often I was reluctant to obey—somewhat like Moses. But I take comfort when I read how Jesus himself asked that the cup of suffering be withdrawn, if at all possible. Then "nevertheless not my will, but thine, be done" (Luke 22:42, KJV) is the only prayer.

In one of her talks, Elisabeth Elliot tells about watching a border collie perform. As she watched him stop abruptly at the shepherd's command, standing poised for chase, tail in air, quivering all over, she asked the shepherd's wife if the dog understood what was happening. Only the shepherd knew the need of the sheep, the one lagging behind or caught in the brush, or danger ahead.

The shepherd's wife said, "The dog doesn't understand the pattern—only obedience."

When I read that story I knew it was a picture of my life. And the habit of obedience turned me toward my bedroom, where I dressed with trembling fingers and a deep cry in my heart for nick-of-time grace.

As I drove to the church, the Spirit whispered another gentle command when He said, "Now, open your heart and let your Sunday School class walk through your sorrow with you. Don't try to go it alone."

How well He knew the independent side of me. Is there a bit of pride in that approach to life that has to be constantly crucified? I'm afraid so. Born in England with a strong English background, the oldest of six children, living in parsonages, often in poverty, and surviving 14 years of missionary life in India, perhaps I had become too used to the lonely furrow. However, I decided to follow through and teach my class. Before I faced them, I took the cup of Communion imaging all those hostages under the protection of the blood of Jesus. It was a deeply moving time for me. The bread was taken with a prayer for courage to endure whatever the future held. I've never taken Communion since then that this memory doesn't return.

After my rather tear-filled class session, warmth radiated all around me from their loving support, like sunlight after a rain storm. One of the dear members came up to me and said, "I want to share an old Scotch proverb with you. 'You don't thatch your roof when it's raining.'" Thank God, when the storms came I knew where to go for shelter, for a quiet time had been my habit for many years.

Two days after this traumatic Sunday was state election day. I really wasn't too interested in the political contests as my grief was still surrounding me like a cloud. But I remembered the admonition—"Do the next thing"—so off I went to the polling booth. As I walked in the bright sunshine, the Spirit spoke to me another wonderful promise that I was to cling to for many months: "Said I not unto thee, that, if thou wouldest believe, thou shouldest see the glory of God?" (John 11:40, KJV). (It seems most of the Spirit's promptings come to me in the King James Version, with which I have been familiar all my life.) Again, like the border collie, I didn't understand the pattern. I only knew to obey and to trust a wisdom far greater than my own.

From that day on, the center of my praying throughout those months was for God to get glory to His name and for His will to be done. Over and over I claimed a beautiful passage from Ps. 94:19 in *The Living Bible:* "Lord, when doubts fill my mind, when my heart is in turmoil, quiet me and give me renewed hope and cheer."

Three days after the capture, November 7, I was deeply burdened for Gary. I did not know until he came home that it was the date of one of several mock executions he faced. While reading and praying, I came across these words from F. R. Havergal, which I copied into my journal:

> *To Thee I bring my care,*
> *The care I cannot flee.*
> *Thou wilt not only share*
> *But bear it all for me.*
> *Oh, loving Savior, now to Thee*
> *I bring the load that wearies me.*[1]

Under the poem I wrote, "After a long, dark day . . . I fling myself into Thy arms."

Days passed by with a leaden step. My mother-heart was filled with questions of how Gary was. Was he cold and hungry? Tortured? Oh, so many unnerving thoughts. But I also found wonderful comfort in God's amazing grace. I carried on with the daily demands of life—speaking, teaching, cooking, driving, comforting. Through hours of pain too deep for tears, I found it is God's transcendent grace that creates springs in the desert and makes it blossom as the rose. He brings a rift in the clouds. How true are the words from J. H. Jowett: "Our sufficiency is of God, and the oil of grace will keep the lights burning through the longest nights."[2]

As we approached the Christmas season of 1979, every carol, every Christmas tree, every decoration seemed to pierce my heart like a dagger. We sent Christmas presents for Gary to his wife "just in case." It was a tearful shopping time. I firmly believe uncertainty is one of the cruelest of all situations in which to be thrust. How does one survive without faith and hope? Those days I often read the words of that old Christmas song "I Heard the Bells on Christmas Day."

> I heard the bells on Christmas Day
> Their old familiar carols play,
> And wild and sweet the words repeat
> Of peace on earth, goodwill to men.
>
> And in despair I bow'd my head.
> "There is no peace on earth," I said,
> "For hate is strong, and mocks the song
> Of peace on earth, goodwill to men."
>
> Then pealed the bells more loud and deep:
> "God is not dead, nor doth He sleep;
> The wrong shall fail, the right prevail,
> With peace on earth, good will to men."

What a surge of hope these words gave to me in one of the saddest Christmases I had ever known. I thought of the yellow ribbon flying at the top of a smokestack at West Quoddy Head, Maine, where the sun hits the shores of America for the first time. New hope, as well as patriotism, revived my spirit.

Around that time I came across an article by Bob Greene, a syndicated columnist in Chicago. The title of the article was "For Whom the Bells Toll, and Toll Still." He told about a 72-year-old man named Oliver Bilhorn who lived in a crumbling neighborhood in Chicago. On the evening of November 28, 1979, he heard then President Jimmy Carter urge the country's churches to ring their bells each noontime as a sign that the hostages were not forgotten. The next day Oliver Bilhorn walked to a dead-and-forgotten church that had a belfry and a bell, and precisely at noon he began to ring those bells.

Bob Greene writes, "There was no response from anyone in the neighborhood. He went home. The next day at noon he went back. And the day after that. And the day after that." He closed the article with these words:

> Winter is coming. Soon the streets of the neighborhood will be deep with snow; the residents who do go outside in the warm months will spend more and more of their hours behind locked doors.
>
> But every day, on a block where no one is listening, the bells will ring out 52 times. It is a dead church with no pastor and no congregation in a small pocket of the country that has long been forgotten. But at noon, listen to Oliver Bilhorn's bells—they sing an American song.[3]

Can you imagine how I felt? With my eyes filled with tears and deeply moved in my spirit, I decided to write Bob Greene and thank him for that moving article. Not too many days later I received a phone call from him. He said he was so surprised that in the midst of my personal grief I found time to thank him for sharing that story. I told him that during the dark days in which we were living, there were not many uplifting happenings, but it warmed my spirit to think of that dear, elderly man trudging into that old church and ringing those bells of hope. I asked him to please let Mr. Bilhorn know how we felt, which he promised to do. Later we wrote Mr. Bilhorn a personal letter but never received an answer.

On January 16, 1981, Bob Greene wrote another article about our warm conversation on the phone, which ran as a syndicated column in a number of newspapers. The headline read, "A Story of Strength and Courage from a Hostage Family." Included in the column were these words:

"I don't know in all of history if there has been a group of people more prayed for. If anything good has come out of this whole ordeal, it is the feeling that Americans really do care for each other."[4]

Earl and I knew prayers were being prayed around the clock as our tapes from First Church were literally circling the earth. Every so often the wonderful choir at First Church sang a special song for me, with the words "Hold on, my child—joy comes in the morning." I still weep inside anytime I hear it sung. For I kept holding on—holding to God's uplifting hand.

If you've knelt beside the rubble of an aching, broken heart,
When the things you gave your life to fell apart;
You're not the first to be acquainted with sorrow, grief, or pain.
But the Master promised sunshine after rain.

To invest your seed of trust in God in mountains you can't move,
You risk your life on things you cannot prove;
But to give the things you cannot keep for what you cannot lose
Is the way to find the joy God has for you.

Hold on, my child, Joy comes in the morning,
  Weeping only lasts for the night;
Hold on my child, Joy comes in the morning,
  *The darkest hour means dawn is just in sight.**

Chapter 7

The Homecoming

J oy Comes in the Morning!" How often the words to that song brought a longing to my heart. Someone has said that anticipation can be greater than realization. But it was the opposite for us—believe me. The weekend before the hostages were released, I had gone to speak for a ladies' retreat. I remember the apprehension I felt as I packed my suitcase, fearful that perhaps I would miss the television coverage of the hostages' release. Things were coming to a climax. I was going to a retreat center where there was no television and very limited, poor radio reception. But the Spirit once more whispered to me, "You'll never miss a thing."

It was a delightful retreat, and I came home to a houseful of reporters Earl had welcomed into our home. I was flabbergasted. The excitement everywhere was beyond description. We spent hours glued to the television. The air was saturated with hope and anticipation.

It was January 20, 1981, my birthday, when we saw Gary for the first time after months of uncertainty and concern. The hostages were photographed getting off the plane in Algeria, looking weary and bedraggled. In my heart I wondered if Gary's mind had been affected as I saw the pain in his eyes when he turned toward the camera. Then as he walked away, he raised his right arm in a gesture of defiant victory—and I knew he was all right. Tears of relief were everywhere as the entire family clustered together. We took off the prayer bracelets we had been wearing for weeks and laid them on the coffee table. Our prayers had been answered.

That night as we waited for a possible telephone call from Gary, I told Earl I felt an assurance that Gary would be OK mentally if, when he called us, he spoke to Earl in Marathi, the language we had learned in India. About 2 A.M. the phone rang, and I heard Earl answer Gary in Marathi. I raced to the phone in the study, and we had a loving conversation with him. His voice was hoarse from his long calls to his family in Falls Church, Va. It was a moving moment when, at the close of our phone visit, we three prayed the Lord's Prayer together—he in Weisbaden, Germany, and we in Pasadena. Indeed, joy came that morning.

The newspaper coverage of the hostages' release was poignant and colorful. Here are a few excerpts:

> It was an extraordinary, unforgettable moment in the nation's history: a week-long, yellow-ribboned-wrapped outpouring of pride, patriotism, and joy. Our hostages were home, and we were one again.
>
> They rode one last time through the blacked-out streets of Tehran. Their buses and vans slipped into the Mehrabad Airport through a sealed-off back gate, and they spilled out into the moonlit tarmac looking dazed and lank-haired in their motley assortment of denim, sandals, and ill-fitting fatigues. They endured one last torment between them and the waiting Air Algerie 727—a forced march past a gauntlet of militants raining kicks and curses. And then they were aboard—the runway lights blazed on, and at 12:25 P.M. RST on Tuesday, January 20, the jet roared aloft bearing the 52 hostage Americans on their long night's journey into day.[1]

Even now as I type this account after many years, my heart is full of remembered emotion. We asked Gary sometime later for his memory of the night of his release, and he told us the hostages had no idea they were being released. They thought they were being taken out to be executed. They were told to leave their personal effects in a bundle on their cots—he left his Bible, the Jowett meditation book,

46

and our book, *The Cycle of Victorious. Living*, wrapped together. (He later received these things through the Red Cross.)

Gary told us he counted every rivet on the steps to the plane, thinking he would soon be dead. They were told nothing as they sat silently in the plane for fear the Iranians might still pull some cruel trick out of their sleeves. After they flew out of Iranian airspace toward Algeria, they were then told they were on their way home. Can you imagine the eruption of joy on that plane? The euphoria lasted for days. Gone were mock executions, confinement in basement cells, being tied to their chairs, being blindfolded and unable even to see each other, being shoved into vans and then into various prisons, no mail from home, solitary confinements—the full story of their ordeal has never been fully revealed.

Gary told us that during his solitary confinement he was fed watery soup and a cup of tea each day. No wonder he lost 40 pounds. One day he put a bit of sweet tea on the floor of his cell, and a little parade of ants came in. Something alive was a relief during the long days. Every afternoon he looked forward to his "little friends." Then they finally quit coming, and he was all alone. He played golf in his mind with his father and built a wooden deck on the back of his house, nailing each board and gauging the width and length all in his mind. The deck is there now just as he envisioned it.

Before Gary was released, I read a quote from Aleksandr Solzhenitsyn, who knew all about imprisonment. He wrote chapters of his books mentally while imprisoned. He said that when he was in prison, every part of his body changed, molecule by molecule. He added that one is never the same again. You can readily see why we had much apprehension about Gary's mental state, which did remain healthy, thanks to God.

On the day of Gary's release the eruption of joy in Pasadena, and especially around the parsonage, was beyond words. Front door, back door, in the house, and the backyard—reporters everywhere—balloons, tattered American flags that had flown for over a year, yellow ribbons that had been around oak trees and palm trees and on mailboxes and car antennas, etc., were brought along with food and flowers. I still have a trunk full of these mementos—how to discard them, these symbols of joy?

A troop of little Brownies had brought me a birthday cake. I went outside to cut the cake, and we all stood together on the sidewalk (no room in the house), laughed, and ate together. If the measure of grief can equal the measure of joy, our joy reached to the heavens.

One week later, on January 27, we flew to Washington, D.C., on American Airlines Flight 10, called "Freedom Flight," to welcome our son home. He had met his immediate family at West Point; now it was our turn. On a cold gray morning we boarded a bus near our hotel for the exciting ride to Andrews Air Force Base. I remember our daughter-in-law, Linda, saying, "I feel all red, white, and blue." She expressed how we all felt.

When we arrived at the base we were placed behind a red rope and politely asked not to cross over the line when the plane came in. We were told the hostages would be coming in on four planes. As I strained my eyes to see the first one outlined in the sky, I wondered which one Gary would be on. After the first plane circled and landed, I watched eagerly as the door opened. First then Vice President George Bush, his wife, Barbara, and pilot Colonel Schaeffer and his family stepped out.

And there, to our amazement, was Gary and his family. Tears filled my eyes as I saw him waving and smiling. But the red cord was too much for my long-legged husband, who leaped over it and ran toward his son, who had been "lost" but now was found. Their reunion reminded me of the great day when we shall all be united with our Heavenly Father and hear those wonderful words, "Well done, good and faithful servant!" We who looked on were a cloud of witnesses to a joyful reunion. Then our turn came for the exquisite joy of touching and hugging our loved one.

Soon we boarded the buses for the ride back to the White House. Thousands of Americans were responding with deep patriotism to these returning hostages. Gary sat in front of us, leaning out the window as he held the little flags thrust into his hand, saying over and over in a hoarse voice, "Thank you; thank you." I saw older men stand with their hats over their hearts, probably remembering another type of war they had fought and won; posters held high in the air saying, "We love you; God bless you"; yellow ribbons on baby bonnets; people making victory signs with their hands, crowding the streets and balconies along Pennsylvania Avenue.

Kathryn Koob later remarked, "Today is like taking a bath in love—we soaked in it for hours." Haynes Johnson of the *Washington Post* wrote, "It became a day of spontaneous national celebration unmatched in many years." One poster said, "Freedom—how sweet it is!" "America's joy pealed from church belfries, rippled from flag staffs, and wrapped itself in a million miles of yellow ribbon . . ."[2]

As we drove through this frenzy of joy past LaFayette Square on to Pennsylvania Avenue into the great Circle Drive to the White House, we saw marines standing at attention. Everyone was responding with appreciation to these hostages. They were not heroes, but patriots who had done their duty well and refused to bow in submission to an outlaw nation. They kept their integrity.

I could hardly contain my own feelings when we walked into the White House and heard the Marine Band playing "Tie a Yellow Ribbon 'Round the Old Oak Tree." How often that song had brought a pang to my heart throughout that 444-day ordeal. Memories do bless and burn. How true.

As we went out to the South Lawn, we brushed shoulders with all of Washington's dignitaries, recognizing many of them. The platform where the hostages stood to be welcomed was rimmed with American flags. The atmosphere was electric with joy. But all we had eyes for was one thin young man in the front row who had come safely home. The newly-elected President greeted them with words from Psalm 126 (KJV): "The Lord hath done great things for us; whereof we are glad." This made my cup of joy overflow, for we knew it was prayer that created this miracle of freedom.

One year later in February, when Gary and family were visiting us, he had an interview with a reporter from the *Los Angeles Times*. By then Gary had spoken all over the country in schools and churches, as well as at government functions; he had written scores of letters to school children thanking them for their support; he had received many honors and a medal from the State Department. He came to thank the people of Pasadena First Church again for their support—and to celebrate his birthday.

The headline on the reporter's article read, "Father's Church Gave Him Hope." He told the congregation, "Thank you for creating a miracle. Many people thought miracles ended years ago. I thought so too. But a miracle is what happened to the American people. The hostages were the catalyst that brought the country together. That's a miracle that God created." He added that his relationship with God was a deep and personal one. He said he and a group of hostages who were imprisoned together at one time had religious discussions.

"Those of us in that room came to the general conclusion that either Jesus was the greatest 'shyster' that ever hit this planet or He was the Son of God," Gary explained. "We collectively agreed that He had to be the Son of God." Then he closed with these words: "You can't take the Christian religion without the life of Christ in it. There was a Christ historically, and He's alive today. If you don't want to believe that, you have to find another religion."

It is now 1992. More hostages have been taken and returned. These are difficult days for the American people. Gary has faced cancer surgery but seems in good remission. He probably will be retiring from the State Department in a year. He is working on a master's degree at George Washington University in preparation for another career. For all of us, his year in captivity leaves scars, wounds, and healing. As I review this experience, I feel a special rapport with a few lines from Rudyard Kipling in his poem "Recessional."

> *The tumult and the shouting dies;*
> *The Captains and the Kings depart:*
> *Still stands Thine ancient sacrifice,*
> *An humble and a contrite heart.*
> *Lord God of hosts, be with us yet,*
> *Lest we forget—lest we forget!**

* Emphasis added.

Chapter 8

Lessons from the Petoskey Stone

I presume not too many people besides those who live in Michigan would know much about these very unusual stones. I first heard about these stones from a book titled *Polishing the Petoskey Stone,* by Luci Shaw, a contemporary Christian poet. It was sent to me by a dear friend, Gunnell Jorden. After reading about this stone and becoming quite intrigued, I found out we were to have a retreat in Petoskey, Mich.

As soon as we had some free time, we drove into the quaint gaslight section of the village, and I looked for a Petoskey stone. As we drove through the winding streets I spied a little shop called "The Petoskey Stone Shop." It was full of these fascinating stones, and I bought one that had been polished by a master craftsman. With it was a little folder that told in more detail about the origin of the craft.

I've been told these stones are found in no other place of the world except along the shores of Lake Michigan in the lower peninsula of Michigan. It was made Michigan's state stone June 28, 1965. It is a fossilized colony coral tracing its origin back to the Devonian Seas that scientists say covered the lower peninsula millions of years ago. These stones consist of massive corals of varying sizes and shades that, when wet, disclose scores of tiny shell-like rings—the marks of prehistoric marine life that has been petrified, according to geologists. When dry, the stones are silvery with no apparent markings. There are no two stones alike, although they have a similar look.

Before me as I type are three phases of these stones. One is in its rough state, with extremely faint markings. Another has been rubbed smooth but with no polish, and the third has been highly polished by a master craftsman. As I studied about these stones (after reading Luci Shaw's poem), I saw a beautiful analogy, which I shared with the ladies in our women's session.

These stones all look alike and are difficult to distinguish from other dull, gray, mostly round shore stones. I spent at least an hour one very cold, windy day searching for a stone of my own but never found one. One that I have is a gift from one of the preacher's wives who went out looking for them after our session.

Basically, human beings all look alike, but in God's sight we are each unique and very special. The potential for beauty is in every living soul. But the secret for revealing the inner beauty is to allow the Master Craftsman, God our Creator, to do the polishing—and *the stone has to be wet!*

The exquisite beauty God sees in His children can become a reality only through our tears. He never needlessly causes His children pain, but life and its unsought-for circumstances are not respecters of persons. We all weep. God puts our tears in a bottle like the alabaster gift of Mary of Bethany. Not one tear is unseen by our loving Lord, and "for those tears He died." Only in heaven will we weep no more.

I have a card from Luci Shaw, who wrote *God in the Dark* following the death of her husband. I wrote to thank her and told her about a latch-hook rug I had worked on during the year Gary was a hostage in Iran. Into that rug went many tears, as well as prayers of trust and thanksgiving for the Comforter during those dark days. She sent me a card she had used as a Christmas greeting, and on the front was the word "Quiltmaker." After reading my letter, she said I might appreciate the words of a prairie woman who in 1870 wrote about her quilts—"I make them warm to keep my family from freezing; I make them beautiful to keep my heart from breaking!"

My latch-hook rug filled those empty spaces in grief—when the mind idles and the heart is still. The last lines of the poem read:

> She pieced them beautiful and summer-bright,
> to thaw her frozen soul. Under her fingers
> the scraps grew to green birds, and purple,
> improbable leaves; deeper than calico, her mid-winter
> mind burst into flowers. She watched them bloom
> between the double stars, the wedding rings.*

Have we not all found a strange solace during grief when we do something with our hands? The exertion is therapy, it seems. I washed windows and cried all day when my father died. I wept with the falling snowflakes and wrapped Christmas presents during a family divorce. Grief is such a lonely road except for His golden presence.

I told the women at the retreat that when Gary was released I put the rug aside and have not been able to finish it—too many painful memories. But after the session, a dear lady came to me, offered to finish it, and suggested I send it to my son. What a healing balm her thoughtfulness was, and is, to me.

The beautiful thing about this polishing that life and God give to us is its purpose. It is for the display of *His splendor* that we might shine as lights in this dark, dark world. How often we have read the statement, "The chief end of man is to glorify God and to enjoy Him forever." When we face all the things we do not understand but allow Him to "sanctify to us our deepest distress," we bring glory to His name.

It takes time to polish a stone, but after the gloss is achieved, "the surface is semi-transparent; that is, when

* Reprinted from *Polishing the Petoskey Stone,* © 1990 by Luci Shaw. Used by permission of Harold Shaw Publishers, Wheaton, Ill.

the stone is burnished smooth as glass you can see deep into it, as if to its 'soul,' and feel that it is looking back at you, as each of us looks back at God with our inner eyes when we sense He is focusing in on us." Luci Shaw continues: "I feel like a Petoskey stone, once gray and dull, but now achieving a gloss that shows it for what it is. And I know who is doing the polishing."[1]

There is a time in our pilgrimage when we become transparent—no hidden agenda, no closed doors, no strings attached. The ego becomes crucified daily, and we constantly take sides against our human self and desires so that we might walk a higher road and know a deeper joy that is "unspeakable and full of glory." We learn to "let those that we love go to Jerusalem," as Oswald Chambers says. Sometimes this process causes the deepest tears. Even so, there are experiences in life "too deep for tears"—but the gloss is already on the stone.

The other day I was deep in prayer for several personal family matters. I asked God for a word of comfort. The Holy Spirit directed me to read in my usual Old Testament portion for the day. I decided to obey the prompting, although I was dubious I would find much in Exodus. I turned to the second chapter and read about the birth of Moses. What an unusual story! With what tears his mother must have woven the little ark-cradle for her beautiful little son, and yet with what faith as well. Her plan to have Miriam, his sister, nearby showed a quiet trust that whoever found the little baby would need a nursemaid. But my real comfort came from a footnote in the *Amplified Bible* by F. B. Meyer. He writes:

> They launched the ark not on the Nile only, but on God's providence. He would be captain, steerman, and convoy of the tiny bark. Miriam stood to watch. There was no fear of fatal consequences, only the quiet expectancy that God would do something worthy of Himself. They reckoned on God's faithfulness and they were amply rewarded, when the daughter of their greatest foe became the babe's patroness.[2]

It was the baby's tears that caught at the heart of the princess, and Miriam, hiding nearby, stepped out to offer her mother, Moses' mother, to care for the little one. Can you imagine the joy in Jochebed's heart to hold her little son in her arms again, to nurse him, and to even be paid for such exquisite joy. How our Father loves to do over and abundantly beyond our dreams as a reward to our faith.

But to continue to trust when the days are bleak and barren and there seems no light in the darkness must bring a special joy to our lord. At such times we trust in the character of God and His priceless, unfailing love, regardless of what we realize as answer to our prayers. His ultimate will shall prevail.

As we read John's vision in the Revelation, we find hope for all our future in chapter 21, verses 1, 3, and 4:

> Then I saw a new heaven and a new earth, for the first heaven and the first earth had passed away, and there was no longer any sea. . . . And I heard a loud voice from the throne saying, "Now the dwelling of God is with men, and he will live with them. They will be his people, and God himself will be with them and be their God. He will wipe every tear from their eyes. There will be no more death or mourning or crying or pain, for the old order of things has passed away."

Chapter 9

"The Clerk of the Works"

In the 1970s Azusa Pacific University had a pastoral seminar, and I chose to enroll. The speakers were from several different denominational backgrounds, which added a delightful flavor. One of the speakers was a Salvation Army colonel, and he spoke with a warm heart and from vast experience. One statement he made planted itself deep into my heart and mind. He referred to the Holy Spirit as "the Clerk of the Works." This immediately fascinated me, even though I had no idea of the meaning of the phrase or even its application. Colonel Neufeld had a delightful English accent, and "clerk" sounded like "clark," which is the way an Englishman would say it and hear it. Fine!

The phrase "clerk of the works" did not catch my attention again until we were in England and were visiting the famous Salisbury Cathedral. As we entered the courtyard, we saw a temporary workers' shed for tools and other items. Hazel was ahead of me and, with a great deal of excitement, called to me and said, as she pointed to a sign on the shed, "Look! The Clerk of the Works!" But we didn't see anyone around.

In the process of visiting the 12th-century cathedral, we had a retired military man as our guide. During the tour, on a Good Friday, all visitors were asked to pause at noon and make a special prayer. The quiet in that huge cathedral was unforgettable. Later, I saw a plaque on a wall as a memorial to a man who had been clerk for 50 years. I then asked our guide if they had a present clerk of the works on the job.

Pointing to some scaffolding on one side of the edifice, he said, "Oh, yes. This clerk has been on the job 17 years." I was impressed but ignorant. Yet I sensed a spiritual truth hidden in this experience.

Soon we were on our tour bus to continue our journey through lovely England. Right in the seat in front of me was my special friend, Robert Parker, an architect and builder in his own right. "Robert, help me!" I said: "We have seen the title 'the Clerk of the Works.' Who is he? What is he?" While hardly catching a breath, Robert gave the connecting link to a gold mine.

"The clerk of the works is the person on the project full time," he said. "His purpose is to see that everything done on the building site is in accordance with what the designing architect intended. He is paid by the owner, but he is the official representative of the architect."

Enter the Clerk of the Works—the Holy Spirit! The Architect introduced Him to our world.

Jesus told us very clearly in John 14:26—"But the Counselor, the Holy Spirit [the Clerk of the Works], whom the Father will send in my name, will teach you all things and will remind you of everything I have said to you." Now this is a tall order for the Clerk of the Works, but He is committed to fulfilling every detail of this assignment.

It is clear that one of the major assignments of the Clerk of the Works is to direct us to Jesus—also known as "the author and perfecter of our faith" (Heb. 12:2). His total emphasis is to uphold Jesus. His work is always in the background, and His deepest work is with our attitudes. It is just as our son Grant stated while in the depths of studying for his graduate degree: "Dad, I am convinced that the deepest work of the Holy Spirit is in the area of attitudes." We can quickly relate this meaningful statement to Gal. 5:22-23. Let us think of these words as a photograph of the Clerk of the Works—the Holy Spirit: "But the fruit of the

Spirit is love, joy, peace, patience, kindness, goodness, faithfulness, gentleness and self-control." Here is a picture of the area the Holy Spirit works in the most.

Later, on another trip to the Salisbury Cathedral, I had an opportunity to meet the clerk of the works personally. I had asked directions to his office. Several "NO NOT EN-TER" signs did not hinder my pursuit, and eventually, after a knock on his office door, I was in. After a brief handshake and snapshot, I was aware he was too busy for me.

Oh my! Not so with the Clerk of the Works of the Divine Personhood—He is always available. No detail is too small for Him. He never tires of my coming, my slowness, or my detours. He "shall guide thee continually" (Isa. 58:11, KJV). The only sign on His office, which is the universe, is one word in every language in our world: "Come," and included would be, "Keep on coming."

Can you begin to see the excitement of this analogy? The idea of the Holy Spirit as the Clerk of the Works has captivated me, and with it has come a deep desire that this thought shall make a conscious penetration into your heart.

The greatest news is not that Jesus, our Architect, introduced the Clerk of the Works—not that He set up the platform for His work, equipped His office, and made all ready for His coming. All this would have been quite important, but the great news, the world-changing news, is "He came! The Clerk of the Works is here"—full time, on the job, bringing every detail desired by the Architect, Jesus Christ, to each of us.

The Clerk burst into our world out of the confines of an office. It all happened in Jerusalem according to the divine blueprint. Jesus ascended into heaven, but a group of ordinary men and women took Jesus seriously, and our world has never been the same since. Those 120 men and women were totally committed to the Clerk of the Works— filled with the Holy Spirit—and they erupted out of the Upper Room not only to shock a world but to begin a healing touch that to this day is still moving. Acts 2:4, says, "All of them were filled with the Holy Spirit and began . . ." We fill in the blanks as the Clerk brings every detail and possibility right into the center of our lives. I love what William Barclay says:

> The Christian is a man who is dyed through and through with the Spirit. He is a man whose whole life is soaked in the Spirit, a man the color of whose whole life is changed by the Spirit. The Christian is a Spirit-anointed, Spirit-dipped, Spirit-saturated, Spirit-dominated man. And the drabness of life, and the inadequacy of life, and the futility of life, and the earth-boundness of life which characterize so many of us, all come from the failure to submit to the baptism of the Spirit which Christ alone can give.[1]

Can you begin to understand why I wanted you to meet the Clerk of the Works? Since retirement, instead of having a pastoral ministry, we have been blessed with the honor of traveling our world into the Church everywhere. Oh, how we need—must have—the Clerk of the Works, the Holy Spirit, in complete charge of His creation, the Church. He brings that extra, that contagion, that overflow, that mighty drawing power of God himself. As my friend John Henry Jowett prayed,

> May the Holy Spirit make my faith and hope invincible. The best service which can be rendered me is not to change my circumstances, but to make me superior to them. Not to make a smooth road but to enable me to "leap like an hart" over any road. Not to remove the darkness, but to make me "sing songs in the night." And so I will not pray for less burden but for more strength![2]

This is the gracious ministry of the Comforter—the Clerk of the Works.

Chapter 10

The Will of God!

For most of us this is a common subject. Of course we know *about* the will of God—and even *know* the will of God. After all, am I not a teacher or even a preacher or a missionary or, let's say, a carpenter? Then I think, "Really, these are all things in life I do."

In New Zealand I heard a classic on the will of God: "The will of God is a fine thing, but you don't wait for it as much as you join in on the doing of it." As I contemplate this statement I feel a movement, an on-goingness in the heart of God toward me, and with it an excitement.

We read statements about the will of God in various places, but none are more gripping than the words of Jesus in Matt. 7:21: "Not everyone who says to me, 'Lord, Lord,' will enter the kingdom of heaven, but only he who does the will of my Father who is in heaven." This utterance seems simple at the outset, but as we get into the heart of the truth, it is quite profound. And yet, as we look into this passage, we are not given a specific "this is the will of God."

Albert Day jolts us a bit as he states, "How often do you and I proclaim the 'will of God' when in fact we have manipulated God into being a cheerleader for our point of view."[1]

Will comes from an original word that carries feeling, even passion. When we say, "What is God's will?" we are asking, "What is God's deep, heartfelt desire for our lives and for our world?" In my search for a specific "this is the will of God," I came into a gold mine. It was while visiting with new believers in the city of Thessalonica that this amazing truth became mine.

Paul's writing to these new Christians is warm, easy to follow, and exciting. They are first-generation Christians who have no hang-ups from previous doctrinal experiences. Paul gives them quite a recommendation in 1 Thess. 2:13: "And we also thank God continually because, when you received the word of God, which you heard from us, you accepted it not as the word of men, but as it actually is, the word of God, which is at work in you who believe."

Paul comes to a clear call in chapter 4 verse 3, when he declares—"This is the will of God, that you should be holy" (NEB). We hold our breath, for Paul is writing to new believers and now calls for them to be holy (set apart—in the world but not of the world—and made clean), and he calls for them to avoid sexual immorality. Paul puts his finger on a very important spot. Yet it is as pertinent today as it was in A.D. 56. Men are men and life is life, the devil is alive and as insistent as ever. He is never creative, yet always persistent. Paul urges these new friends in the thriving city at the crossroads of the commercial world to "be alert and self-controlled" (1 Thess. 5:6).

Paul is closing out this special letter when God's light came on as to the "will of God." In chapter 5, Paul is giving very practical suggestions to the new church, advice on how to live together in harmony, and as he moves on to the power, simplicity, and practicality of the "will of God," he grasps our attention with amazing power. First Thess. 5:16 says it for me and many other liberated souls: "Be joyful always; pray continually; give thanks in all circumstances, for this is God's will for you in Christ Jesus." Paul comes right to the heart of the matter—"for this is God's will for you in Christ Jesus."

To make it personal I outline a triangle:

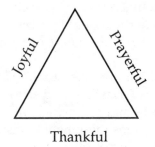

Thankful

It is quite easy to diagram all of this way of life in Christ Jesus. Of course, it is not mine until I lay claim to it. No promise is mine until I put my name on it.

My heart skips a beat. I am so close, and yet in honesty I am stymied by Paul's words "always," "continually," and "in all circumstances." I want to sign up for the "will of God," but really, in my humanness, I am not able to live in such a realm.

The Bible is its own best commentary, and Paul, in writing to a very human group of people in Corinth, makes a statement that takes the pressure off. With it comes freedom. Second Cor. 5:9—"So we make it our goal to please him." Oh, my! Such a surge of joy! I can sign my life over to the will of God all in Christ Jesus, for I qualify! It is my goal to please God by being joyful and prayerful and to give thanks in all circumstances. It was Jowett who said, "Desire is full of holy energy as well as fruition [success]"[2] and "Our goal determines our tendency [destiny]."[3]

I declare myself forever in the will of God. It is not a place or a position as much as a continual way of life. I am under the tutelage—the control—of Christ Jesus. How I am doing in regards to "joyful," "prayerful," "thankful" is between Him and me. He is my resource. The wise man in Proverbs gets me started when he declares, "Joy fills hearts that are planning for good!" (12:20, TLB).

Let us remember that this truth was before theological exposition was a part of our religious world. Wesley, Luther, Calvin, holiness voices, as well as others were not even in the realm of the thought process. It looks as though this idea is right from the heart of God, attended to by Christ Jesus.

But "the half has not been told." He shares great advice with these new Christians and so to thee and me.

In 1 Thess. 5:19 and following, we feel with the Thessalonians as Paul urges these new Christians, "Do not put out the Spirit's fire; do not treat prophecies with contempt. Test everything. Hold on to the good. Avoid every kind of evil." What a way for growth to take place, and what basic church growth factors!

As I feel this passage, as I sit with these friends in Thessalonica, I am amazed at the sweep of the will of God. It is the climax—the payoff to us who are committed, who have signed up for the will of God. "May God himself, the God of peace [Jesus Christ himself], sanctify you through and through. May your whole spirit, soul and body be kept blameless at the coming of our Lord Jesus Christ" (v. 23). Glorious freedom! I am in the will of God, and God promises that He right now sanctifies me as He wished to do, not according to any one theological tradition but according to the God of peace himself. And it will be overwhelming—"through and through"—and He never will get through.

Then the clincher: "The one who calls you is faithful and he will do it" (v. 24). Do what? Sanctify me. Sanctify whom? The person who is in the will of God, who has as his goal to be joyful, prayerful, and thankful, all in Christ Jesus. Relax in Jesus Christ. It is His work.

While pastoring in Pasadena, I made a visit one evening to pray with a member who was to have open-heart surgery the next day. I was sharing some words of encouragement when the young surgeon came in. He was there to encourage my friend, as well as to give an idea of what the surgery would entail. While the surgeon seemed quite relaxed, my friend showed definite signs of tension. I am sure the rehearsal was required. I must confess that I was less than enthusiastic for such a procedure. After a few moments the doctor was gone. My prayer was brief, and I assured my friend I would see him in the morning.

As I drove home I settled some matters. If for any reason I would be the recipient of a surgeon's visit the evening before the operation was to take place and he would begin to give me the plan for surgery, I would politely stop my doctor and ask two major questions. First: "Doctor, have you done this surgery before?" I am sure there would be some chuckles; yet I do not want to be his first as a practicing surgeon. Then, after being assured that I was not number one, my second question would be, "Did the patient live?" On the assurance that the answers to both questions are satisfactory, I would simply smile and, with a toss of my trembling hand, give permission with the words "Go ahead, Doctor."

I think you follow me. "Lord Jesus, dear great Physician, have You done this before? Have You, O God of peace, Jesus, sanctified those who are committed to the will of God? Have You done it before?" A smile from our Lord accompanies a simple statement: "Countless numbers." "And Jesus, did they live?" The quiet response comes across the ages: "Yes—forever and forever and forever."

I am in the will of God. Now I am ready for His *directives.* Now He does guide me, counsel me, and whisper to me, "This is the way; walk in it." Join me in the adventure of being in the will of God.

Chapter *11*

Living with Retirement—
a Form of Relinquishment

According to Dr. Cecil Paul, once president of Eastern Nazarene College, the experience of retiring can be wrapped up in two words: *disengage* and *reinvest*. Easy to say but difficult to do.

After over 18 years of a fulfilling pastorate at Pasadena First Church, we began to realize we were facing another bend in the road. As is often the case, Earl felt it before I did. He realized he was no longer motivated in the pastorate as he formerly had been, and yet there seemed to be some productive years of service left. We began to talk about a possible change.

As was our usual pattern, we did not confer with others but both prayerfully listened to the Holy Spirit. We felt no undue haste, just a quiet listening. It was the spring of 1984, and we had made plans to take a trip to Europe with a group from the Los Angeles District. So we decided to see how we felt after the trip in June.

We put our minds in neutral and had a most enjoyable tour. I was able to visit the little stone house where I was born in Calne, Wiltshire, England. Of course, that was a highlight for me. I guess we all seek our roots sometime in our life, and it is often a moving experience. The courteous resident even let me in to see the little upstairs bedroom where I was born to my 19-year-old war-bride mother.

When we returned from our trip, Earl felt more strongly than ever that he should consider retirement. But when? How to engineer the timing and other details was all a part of our prayers and discussions that summer. But the closer we get to "that certain age," the more questions attack us, like a hive of buzzing bees: where should we live, how close should we be to family, how would we care for an aging parent, what kind of medical coverage would be needed, would finances be adequate, would there be a stimulating challenge ahead, can spouses face each other 24 hours a day without friction, etc.? The retirement age for the Levites was 50, and they often lived well over 100 years with no television, radio, or modern conveniences. Indeed, "committed to grace" seems to be a good motto for retirement.

These are the years in which a durable marriage, based on deep love as well as friendship, spiced up with a sense of humor, is a great blessing. But those who are single, divorced, or bereaved find those years can stretch out like a bleak desert. Learning to live with an outstretched hand of helping love fills up many otherwise empty hours.

Yes, retirement can be like a mirage—shimmering and attractive at a distance but a cold reality when attained. On the other hand, God has plans for senior citizens that have nothing to do with age. The heart's joy, courage, strength, creativity, grace, and fulfillment are all ageless.

For the active pastor, however, in love with his work and his congregation, retirement becomes a form of relinquishment. Perhaps the administrative duties would not be missed, but the sermon preparation with its weekly demand and inspiration and the joy of delivering it would be. And what about following up on the needs of the congregation?—the baby baptisms, the weddings, the comforting of the bereaved, the hospital visitations, the counseling, etc. To some, even that Spirit-directed way of life has to be relinquished. At this stage of life it is good to know that Jesus led us all the way and will continue to lead on in His perfect will.

One of my heaviest concerns was the fact that my

mother, a retired pastor and evangelist, had made her home with us for all of the 18 years we were in Pasadena. It was part of our painful decision, but even so, we knew we had to follow the Holy Spirit's directives.

After weeks of deliberation, we settled on a date two months ahead of our leaving. Earl wrote out his brief resignation, and one Saturday we decided to read it to Mother. I was too upset to go into her room. Tears came to my eyes as I listened outside her door as Earl read what he had written.

I'll never forget my mother's words as I walked into her room. She said, "Don't worry about me. If that is God's will for you, then He has a place for me." She was 87 years old at that time.

Later, as she was out riding with a friend, they drove by a retirement hotel, went in, and found a vacancy with rose-colored carpeting and room for her white bedroom furniture. With financial help from family members, she moved in and has spent the past seven years in a spirit of thanksgiving and contentment in what she feels is her Father's will.

Because of Mother's foresight and prayers, we had a little mountain home, all paid for, in which we could retire. One has to plan for retirement in advance, especially if living in a parsonage. God gave us good sense along that line. We are still enjoying our mountain home at 6,000-foot altitude, where we have blue skies with no smog, along with pine trees, winter snowfalls, and golden fall colors.

Of course we had no assurance at the time we left our fine church what the future held. But our trust was complete in the God who held our future. In the meantime, God gave me this verse from a psalm: "I removed his shoulder from the burden; His hands were freed from the baskets" (81:6, NKJV). I needed that assurance!

After we shared our plans with family, staff, and church, it was amazing how God opened doors for service all over the world. We were astonished. But these opportunities came as a result of the "Cassettes for Christ" ministry described in chapter 2.

Leaving a spacious parsonage with four bathrooms for a small home with one bedroom and one bath was quite an adjustment, especially for me. We had to do a great deal of scaling down by conducting a huge garage sale and donating many things to the Salvation Army. The day our beautiful dining room table went out the door was one of my hardest relinquishments, for I knew family gatherings and entertaining of all types, which I enjoyed, were a thing of the past. Although we were only 60 miles away, I knew each family would be busy in its own activities, and family gatherings in our mountain home would be rare.

As we drove away from the parsonage on a cool December day, my eyes were full of tears, and I did not dare to look back. My tears would have turned me into a pillar of salt, I'm afraid. To make a decision is one thing; to live it out is another. Earl seems to have the happy ability to make his decision firmly and live with it without too many second thoughts. I tend to drag my feet, more apprehensive of the unfamiliar and yet longing to do the right thing.

Because of the impact of the "Cassettes for Christ" ministry, invitations came to us from around the world. To Earl it was an exciting challenge—for me it meant flying. I have never enjoyed flying. I had to find my way through this fear to a reasonable state of rest. I found just praying wasn't enough. I had to fly. The old statement is certainly true: "Courage is fear that has said its prayers." But one step further—you get a ticket, get on the plane, fasten your seat belt, listen to the roar of the engines, take off with sweaty palms, and frantically pray there won't be too much turbulence.

Our first assignment was to Liberia in North Africa, a completely unknown country to us and a long way off. This group of Christians had been without any missionary influence for 30 years. We had two outstanding Spirit-filled weeks with those dear people, in spite of hot Sahara winds, rut-filled roads, different food, and a jam-packed auditorium of hungry listeners to the "Cycle of Victorious Living." One morning we witnessed the baptism of 70 believers, and that night those dear impoverished people gave over $5,000 for the work of their pastors. And so we began a whole new way of life, literally around the world.

But I was struggling with a longing for the familiar. I missed my secure and enjoyable place of being a pastor's wife. I missed teaching my Sunday School class. I missed the joy of sharing in the weekly Bible study. I missed lunches with my daughter, teatime with my mother, and seeing the grandchildren freely. I keenly missed the "shape of Sunday"—Earl's fresh new messages, the beautiful songs from the choir, the friendly warmth of the parishioners. For now I was continually a stranger in a strange land. I seemed to be in a constant state of mourning, and God knew that could not continue.

Three months later we were in Hawaii for a series of meetings. I always enjoy those beautiful islands. The mountains, the exquisite cloud formations, and the balmy air seem to soothe my spirit. I managed the flight over the water with more ease, because I loved where we were going. But I was still struggling inside over retirement. Earl had sent an article into the *Herald of Holiness,* and I squirmed inside as I read the stark truth by his name: "retired elder!" God really needed to do a number on me—and He did.

One morning while in Hawaii, I asked Earl to mail a special postcard for me as he went out for the newspaper. I had written a close friend that Earl seemed to be quite content in this new way of life, but I was having a real struggle. Of course, Earl had the right to read the card, but he usually doesn't bother, so I thought nothing more about it.

That afternoon after we had eaten our meal in a nearby restaurant, out of the blue he leaned toward me and said, "What makes you think I'm content in this retirement?"

I was a bit taken aback at this question, so I asked if he had read my card. He said he had, so I answered him, "Well, you just seem to act that way."

Of course, Earl has always been a positive, optimistic person, but his answer was exactly what I needed to hear. With a most serious intent, he leaned forward and said, "I'll never be content until you are."

So he had read me in spite of my trying to cover up my real feelings. I had work to do, and I turned to the Holy Spirit for new guidance. He gently put His finger on my deepest fault. I needed a purging from past memories that did nothing but create a wistful longing in my spirit. Mentally living over the joys of our parsonage life, especially Sundays, had to be put aside for the time being.

I must confess it was a slow progress, but I had a will set to seize each day and enjoy the moment and be an enjoyable companion to my husband. I don't remember when the pain was relieved, but a time came when my memories were filled with gratitude for the opportunities we had enjoyed—and also a thankfulness for each day ahead, here or afar. I learned to cherish each moment and anticipate the future.

Chapter *12*

The Song Never Ends

In our closing chapters we have shared a few of the insights as well as inspiration from our reading and thinking and praying during these so-called golden years. When we retired eight years ago we had no idea how our loving Father would display to our wondering eyes treasures new and old. Indeed, we could say with the discoverer of King Tut's tomb, "I see wonderful things—wonderful things!"

Perhaps we could call these last few chapters a medley of insights God has given to us in our quiet times, during meditation and prayer—certainly not a symphony, but a strain here and there of celestial music that the Holy Spirit has dropped into our hearts as we look to Him for guidance.

One of Earl's favorite songs to play on his trumpet is "Jesus Led Me All the Way," and deep in our hearts this is our conviction.

> *Jesus led me all the way,*
> *Led me step by step each day;*
> *I will tell the saints and angels*
> *As I lay my burdens down,*
> *Jesus led me all the way.*
>
> *If God should let me there review*
> *The winding paths of earth I knew,*
> *It would be proven clear and true—*
> *Jesus led me all the way.**
>
> —JOHN W. PETERSON

Our song of life has many modulations, of course. There are major and minor chords and rests and pauses, but through it all runs the recurrent theme, "Jesus led me all the way."

It is the summer of 1992 as we write these words, and we have just quietly celebrated our 52nd wedding anniversary. We have planted a golden locust tree in our backyard as our gift to each other, a reminder to us of those wonderful words in Jer. 17:7-8: "But blessed is the man who trusts in the Lord, whose confidence is in him. He will be like a tree planted by the water that sends out its roots by the stream. It does not fear when heat comes; its leaves are always green. It has no worries in a year of drought And *never fails to bear fruit*" (italics added).

As often as we can, we listen to Lloyd Ogilvie's Sunday morning TV program from Hollywood Presbyterian Church. One Sunday he gave us an unforgettable illustration. He was in Scotland feverishly working through the night on a book deadline. The light was on in his study, and a little cleaning woman, who had come to work early, saw it. She tapped on the door, and when he opened it she asked if he would like something hot to drink. He eagerly accepted. As she was turning to leave she asked him, "By the way, Dr. Ogilvie, have you heard God sing today?"

He was taken aback as he answered, "Well, no—as a matter of fact, I haven't!"

Then she reminded him of an amazing scripture in Zeph. 3:17: "The Lord your God is with you, he is mighty to save. He will take great delight in you, he will quiet you with his love, he will rejoice over you with singing." I have so often reminded myself of this beautiful truth when my own song is as feeble as a broken chord.

At another time in my reading I came across a parallel truth:

> We sing, yet not we, but the Eternal sings in us . . . the Everlasting is the Singer . . . the joy we know in the Presence is not our little, private, subjective joy, pocketed away

from other men, a private gift from a benevolent and gracious God. It is the joy and peace and serenity which is in the Divine Life itself, and we are given to share in that joy—the song is put into our mouths, for the Singer of all songs is singing within us. It is not we that sing; it is the Eternal Song of the Other who sings in us, who sings into us, and through us into the world.[1]

The song of redemption is a golden thread from Genesis to Revelation: "the song of Moses and the Lamb." If the chief end of man is to "glorify God and to enjoy Him forever," how more effectively than with singing. Tagore said, "God sees me when I work but He loves me when I sing!"

Although we seldom saw them, we felt that Bob and Peggy Benson were friends of the heart, and it was a deep grief when Bob went to be with his Lord. On the front of the brochure for his funeral service was a picture of Bob and these poignant words:

I used to think,
loving life so greatly,
that to die would be like
leaving the party before the end.

But now I know
that the party is really happening
somewhere else.
That the light and the music escaping in snatches,
to make the pulse beat faster and the tempo quicken,
comes from another place.

And I know, too,
that when I get there,
the music and the love and the praise
will belong to Him,
and the music will never end.[2]

Inside the brochure, under the order of service, were these wonderful, comforting words:

The same Everlasting Father who cares for you today will take care of you tomorrow and every passing day.

Either He will shield you from suffering or He will give you unfailing strength to bear it.

Be at peace then and put aside all anxious thoughts and imaginings.

I am glad the scriptures talk about "songs in the night," for we all face those midnight hours. As the years advance and we become older, there are many "floating anxieties" that could haunt us. We read about the passing of acquaintances of college days and former years and notice the ages in the obituaries, and a sense of our fragile mortality presses in on us. What illness around the corner could pounce on us and change our entire way of life? How long will we be privileged to be together? How will the break come? When? Where?

Yet in spite of statistics and facts that stare us in the face and the chill that could come over our spirits, out of each serious thought comes the promises of God, which wrap themselves around our hearts like a living flame, and we are engulfed in the warmth of hope and anticipation. Jesus told His disciples He was going to prepare a place for them and that He would return and take them to be with Him where He was. I have a quiet belief that when the heavenly home is ready and furnished, He will come "in the fullness of time" and ease us into eternal life.

In her Christmas letter for 1991, Audrey Williamson quoted words from John Greenleaf Whittier that fill the heart with joy:

> *I know not what the future hath*
> *Of marvel or surprise,*
> *Assured alone that life and death*
> *His mercy underlies.*

> And so beside the Silent Sea
> I wait the muffled oar.
> No harm from Him can come to me
> On ocean or on shore.

> I know not where His islands lift
> Their fronded palms in air;
> I only know I cannot drift
> Beyond His love and care.[3]

In one of her former letters, she closed with the phrase, "In His pavilion," and in His pavilion there is light for darkness, joy for sorrow, hope for despair, ease for discomfort, solace for tears, and ever and always the song that never ends—"Lo, I am with you alway, even unto the end of the world" (Matt. 28:20, KJV).

I have found great joy in the words of those who have gone before. George Herbert, an English poet who lived in the 1600s, wrote beautifully about the older years:

> And now in age
> I bud again.
> After so many deaths I
> live and write;
> I once more smell the
> dew and rain
> And relish versing, O
> my only Light.
> It cannot be
> That I am he
> on whom Thy tempests
> fell all night.

None of his poetry was published until after his death—and yet, being dead, he still speaks.

In closing I quote from another poet, the American William Cullen Bryant, in his poem "To a Waterfowl":

> There is a Power whose care
> Teaches thy way along that pathless coast—

The desert and illimitable air—
  Lone wandering, but not lost . . .

* * * *

He who, from zone to zone,
  Guides through the boundless sky thy certain flight,
In the long way that I must tread alone,
  Will lead my steps aright.

And so, we go singing along life's road, confident that the song never ends but will continue into the land of golden day.

Notes

Preface

1. J. H. Jowett, *My Daily Meditation* (LaVerne, Calif.: El Camino Press, 1975), 15.

Chapter 6

1. Leslie D. Weatherhead, *A Private House of Prayer* (Nashville: Abingdon Press, 1958), 107.

2. Jowett, *My Daily Meditation,* 299.

3. Bob Greene, "For Whom the Bells Toll, and Toll Still," Tribune Media Services, 9 December 1980. Reprinted by permission: Tribune Media Services.

4. Bob Greene, "A Story of Strength and Courage from a Hostage Family," Tribune Media Services, 16 January 1981. Reprinted by permission: Tribune Media Services.

Chapter 7

1. "When the Hostages Came Home," *Reader's Digest,* April 1981, 78-84.

2. Ibid. (reference to entire paragraph).

Chapter 8

1. Lucy Shaw, *Polishing the Potoskey Stone* (Wheaton, Ill.: Harold Shaw Publishers, 1990), book jacket. Used by permission.

2. F. B. Meyer, footnote for Exod. 2:4, *The Amplified Bible* (Grand Rapids: Zondervan Publishing House, 1965), 70.

Chapter 9

1. William Barclay, *The Promise of the Spirit* (Philadelphia: Westminster Press, 1960), 25.

2. Jowett, *My Daily Meditation,* 316.

Chapter 10

1. Albert Edward Day, *Day by Day* (Cincinnati: Forward Movement Publications, 1989), June 14 devotional.

2. Jowett, *My Daily Meditation,* 350.

3. Ibid., 357.

Chapter 12

1. Thomas R. Kelly, *A Testament of Devotion* (London: Hodder & Stoughton, 1941), 90.

2. Anonymous poem from book by Bob Benson, *See You at the House* (Nashville: Generoux, Inc., 1986), 1.

3. *Leaves of Gold* (Williamsport, Pa.: Coslett Publishing Co., 1948), 20.